Shit List For

Another Tired-Ass Women

Leaving a five Stars Review in our store will help us create more interesting books for

Tired-Ass Women

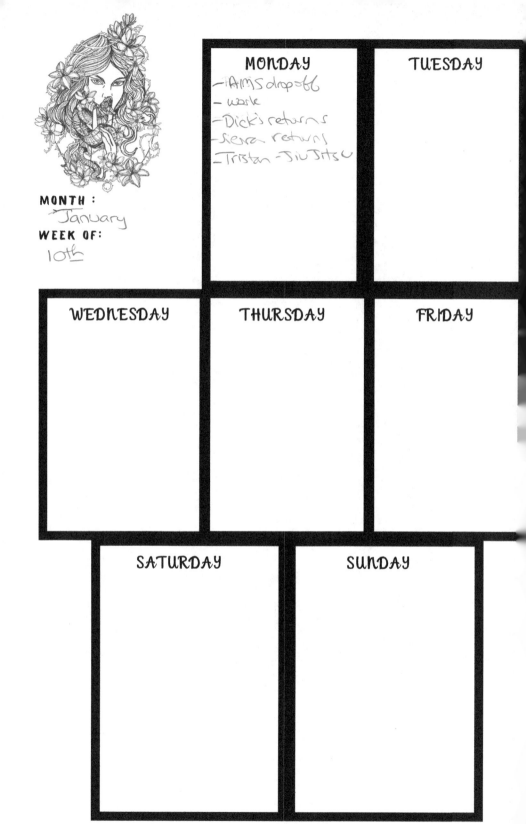

MONTH:
January

WEEK OF:
10th

MONDAY
- AIMS drop off
- work
- Dick's returns
- Sierra returns
- Tristan - Jiu Jitsu

TUESDAY

WEDNESDAY

THURSDAY

FRIDAY

SATURDAY

SUNDAY

This Week's Shit List

- property tax
- prepaid bill
- acdny clm - info $ Subst insurance
- cubseal
- call 'A again? then $Arnold e ash
  Marian re paying Jana

for lunl aedu
My Bac

Other Shit To Remember

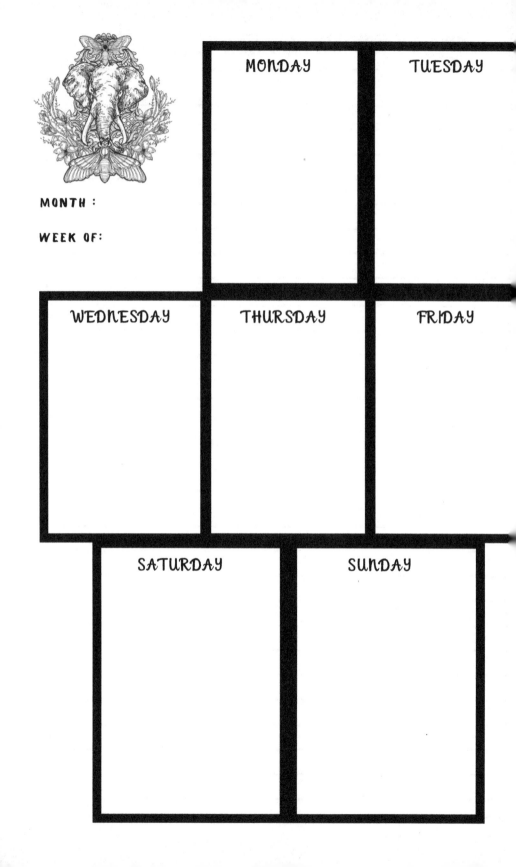

MONTH :

WEEK OF:

MONDAY

TUESDAY

WEDNESDAY

THURSDAY

FRIDAY

SATURDAY

SUNDAY

This Week's Shit List

Other Shit To Remember

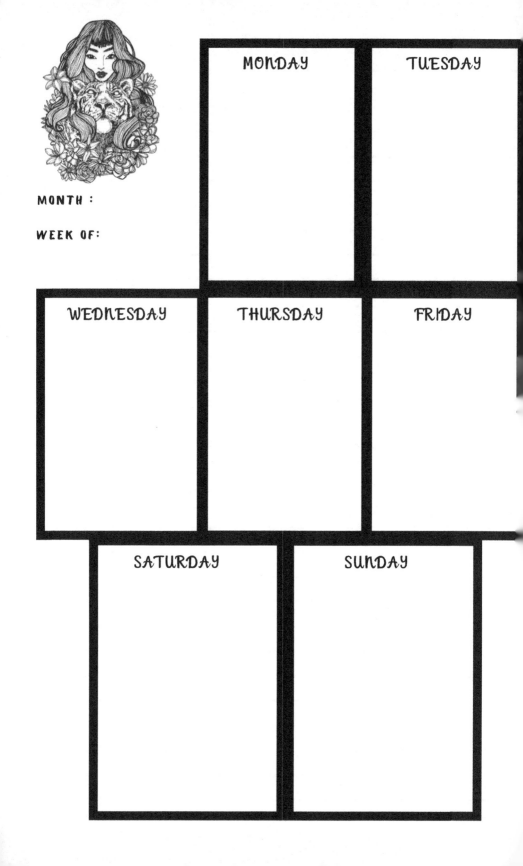

MONTH :

WEEK OF:

MONDAY

TUESDAY

WEDNESDAY

THURSDAY

FRIDAY

SATURDAY

SUNDAY

This Week's Shit List

Other Shit To Remember

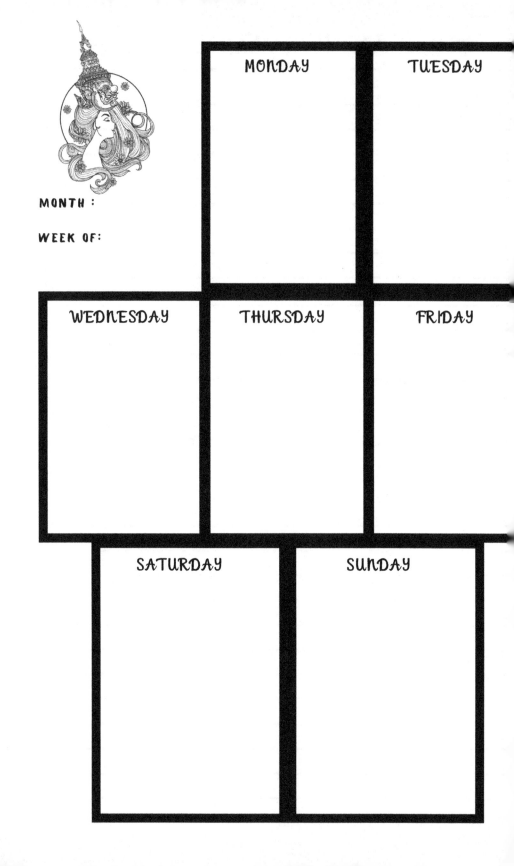

MONTH :

WEEK OF:

MONDAY

TUESDAY

WEDNESDAY

THURSDAY

FRIDAY

SATURDAY

SUNDAY

This Week's Shit List

_____
_____
_____
_____
_____
_____
_____
_____
_____
_____
_____

Other Shit To Remember

_____
_____
_____
_____
_____
_____
_____
_____
_____
_____

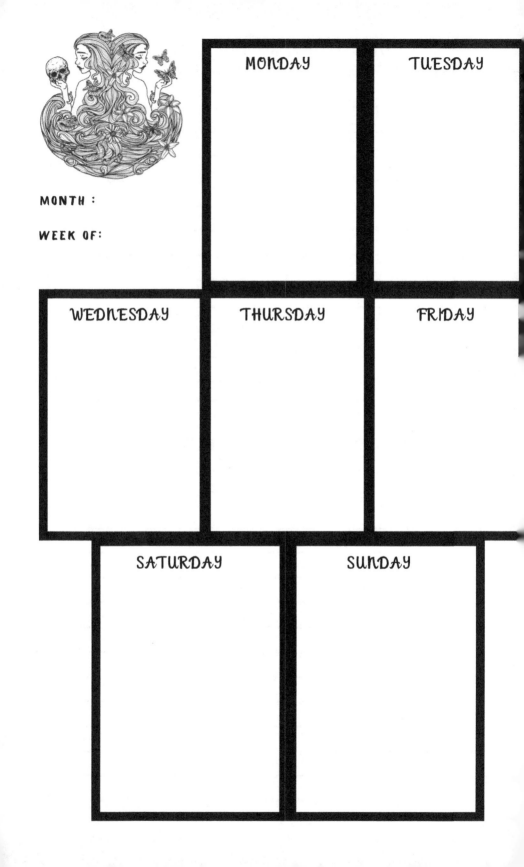

MONTH :

WEEK OF:

MONDAY

TUESDAY

WEDNESDAY

THURSDAY

FRIDAY

SATURDAY

SUNDAY

This Week's Shit List

Other Shit To Remember

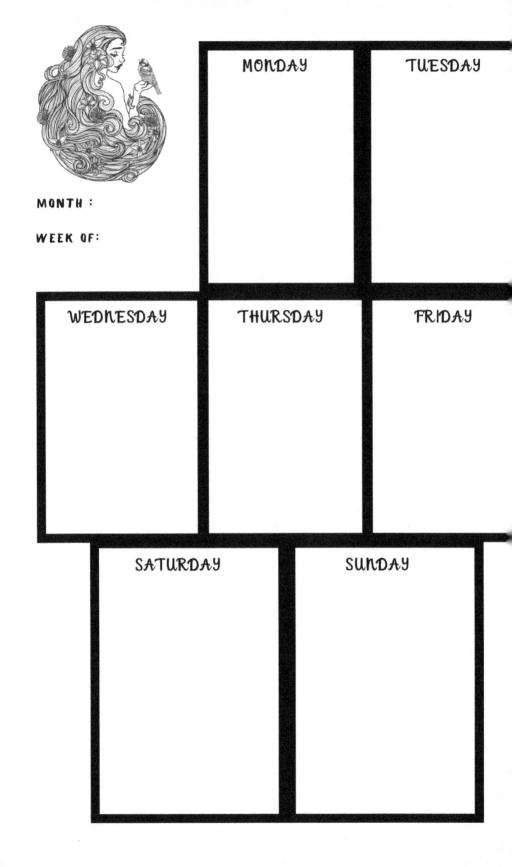

MONTH :

WEEK OF:

MONDAY

TUESDAY

WEDNESDAY

THURSDAY

FRIDAY

SATURDAY

SUNDAY

This Week's Shit List

Other Shit To Remember

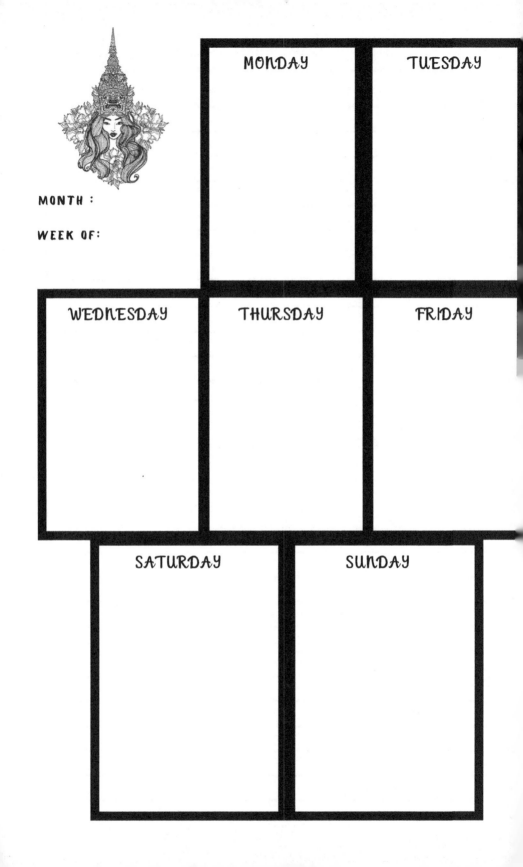

MONTH :

WEEK OF:

MONDAY

TUESDAY

WEDNESDAY

THURSDAY

FRIDAY

SATURDAY

SUNDAY

This Week's Shit List

Other Shit To Remember

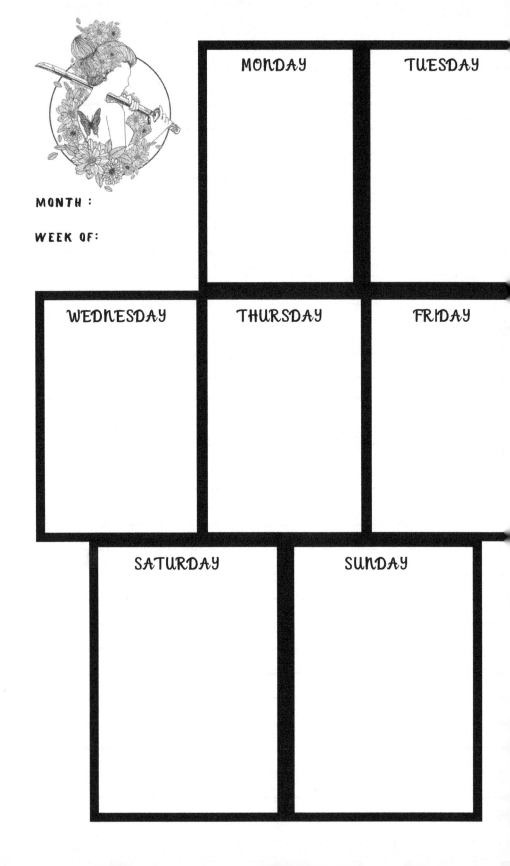

MONTH :

WEEK OF:

MONDAY

TUESDAY

WEDNESDAY

THURSDAY

FRIDAY

SATURDAY

SUNDAY

This Week's Shit List

_____
_____
_____
_____
_____
_____
_____
_____
_____
_____
_____
_____
_____
_____

Other Shit To Remember

_____
_____
_____
_____
_____
_____
_____
_____
_____
_____
_____

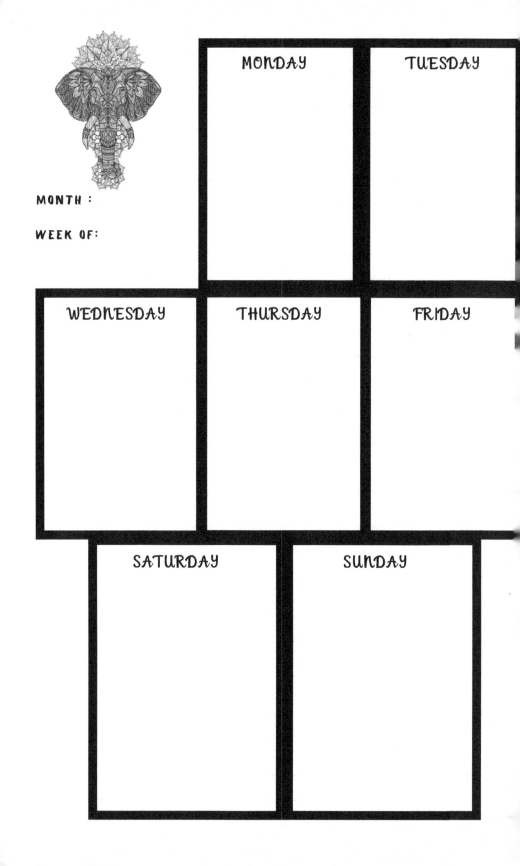

MONTH :

WEEK OF:

MONDAY

TUESDAY

WEDNESDAY

THURSDAY

FRIDAY

SATURDAY

SUNDAY

This Week's Shit List

Other Shit To Remember

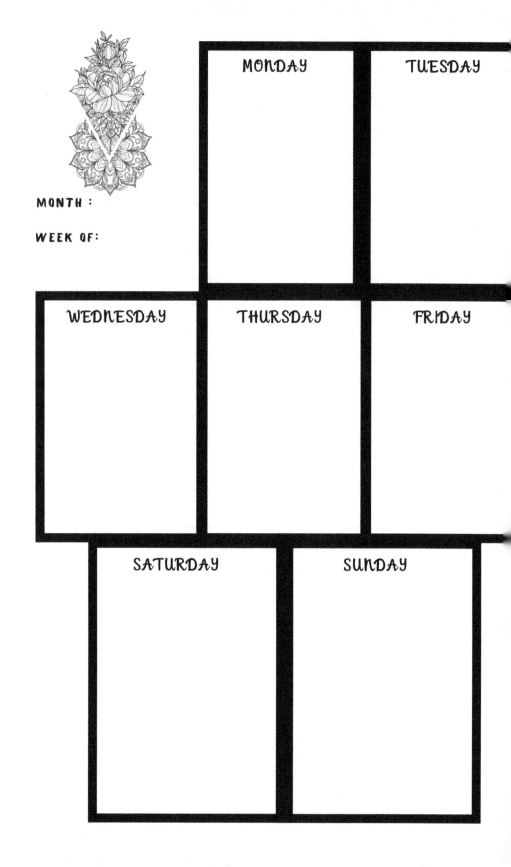

MONTH :

WEEK OF:

MONDAY

TUESDAY

WEDNESDAY

THURSDAY

FRIDAY

SATURDAY

SUNDAY

This Week's Shit List

_____

Other Shit To Remember

_____

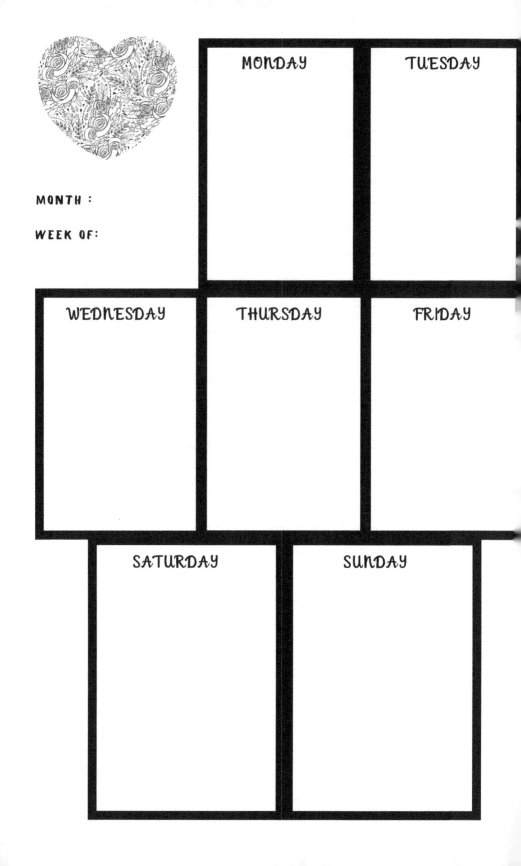

MONTH :

WEEK OF:

MONDAY

TUESDAY

WEDNESDAY

THURSDAY

FRIDAY

SATURDAY

SUNDAY

This Week's Shit List

Other Shit To Remember

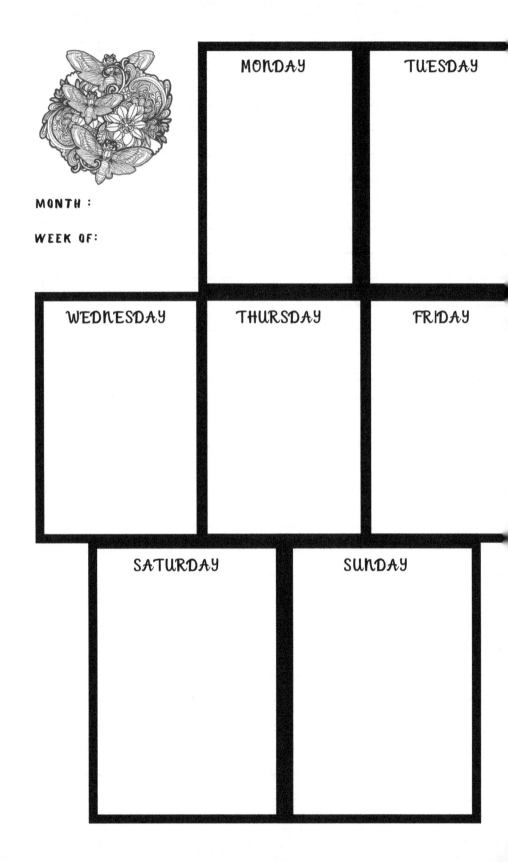

MONTH :

WEEK OF:

MONDAY

TUESDAY

WEDNESDAY

THURSDAY

FRIDAY

SATURDAY

SUNDAY

This Week's Shit List

Other Shit To Remember

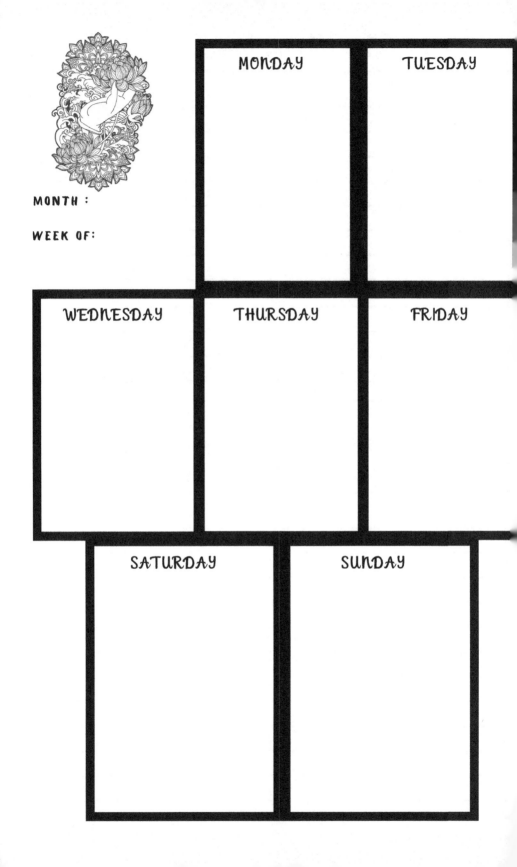

MONTH :

WEEK OF:

MONDAY

TUESDAY

WEDNESDAY

THURSDAY

FRIDAY

SATURDAY

SUNDAY

This Week's Shit List

Other Shit To Remember

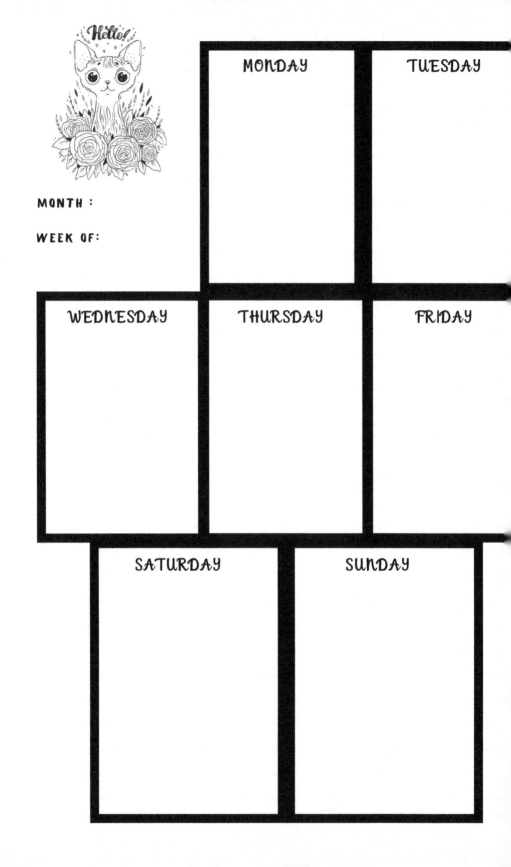

Hello!

MONTH :

WEEK OF:

MONDAY

TUESDAY

WEDNESDAY

THURSDAY

FRIDAY

SATURDAY

SUNDAY

This Week's Shit List

Other Shit To Remember

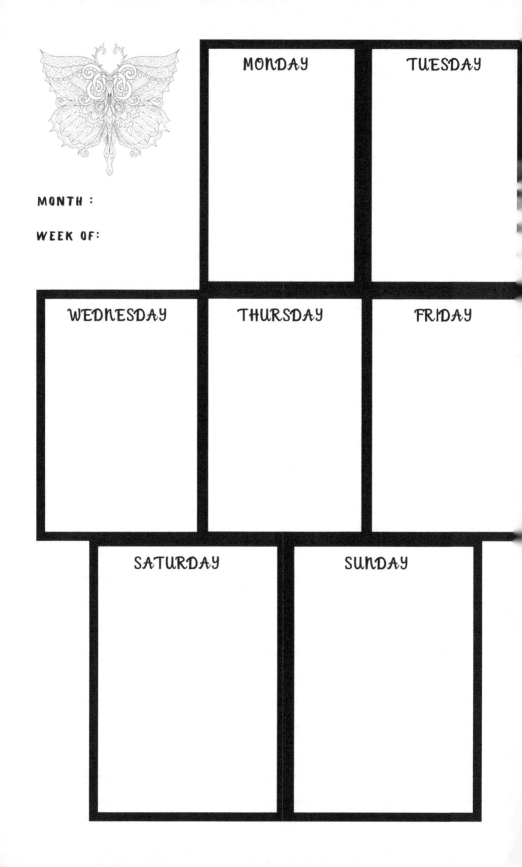

MONTH :

WEEK OF:

MONDAY

TUESDAY

WEDNESDAY

THURSDAY

FRIDAY

SATURDAY

SUNDAY

This Week's Shit List

Other Shit To Remember

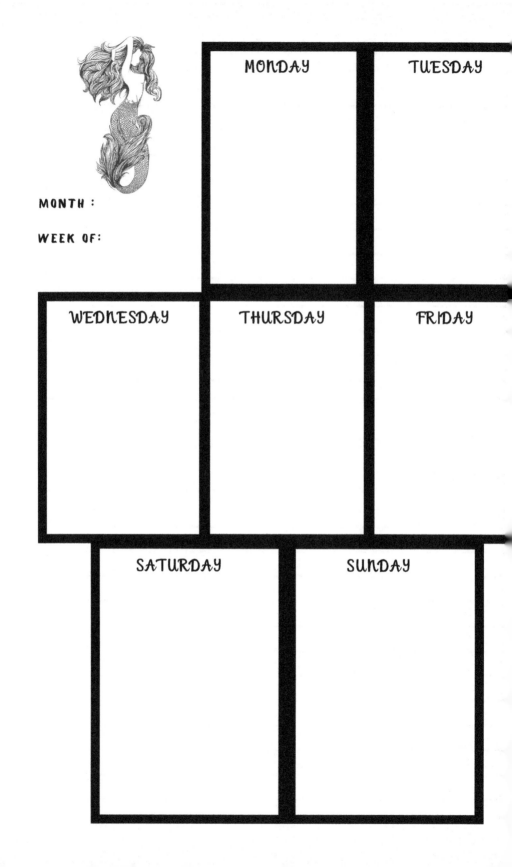

MONTH :

WEEK OF:

MONDAY

TUESDAY

WEDNESDAY

THURSDAY

FRIDAY

SATURDAY

SUNDAY

This Week's Shit List

Other Shit To Remember

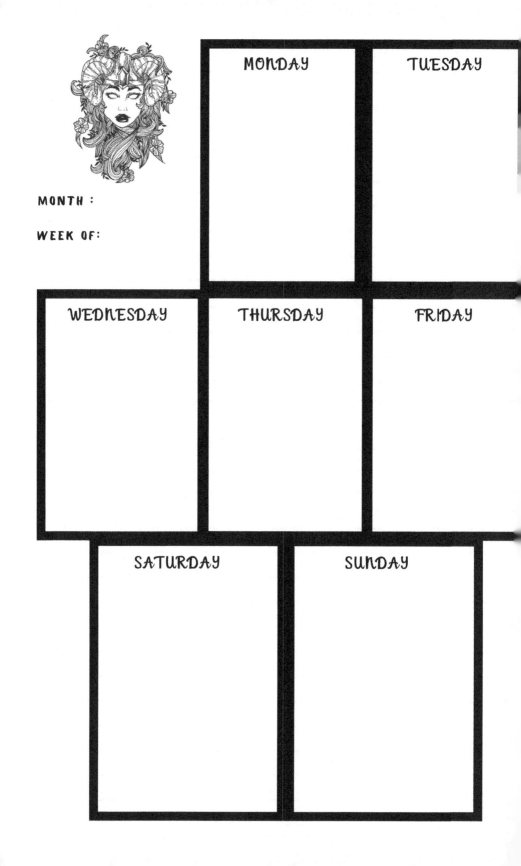

MONTH :

WEEK OF:

MONDAY

TUESDAY

WEDNESDAY

THURSDAY

FRIDAY

SATURDAY

SUNDAY

This Week's Shit List

Other Shit To Remember

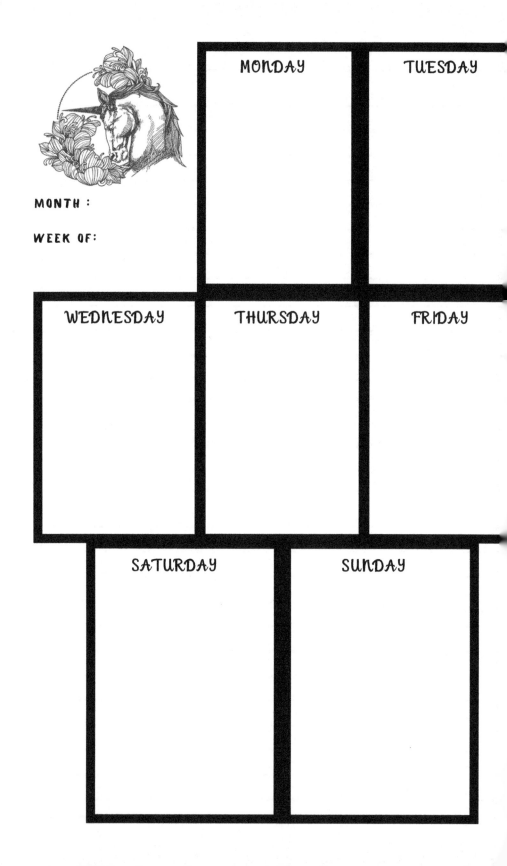

MONTH :

WEEK OF:

MONDAY

TUESDAY

WEDNESDAY

THURSDAY

FRIDAY

SATURDAY

SUNDAY

This Week's Shit List

Other Shit To Remember

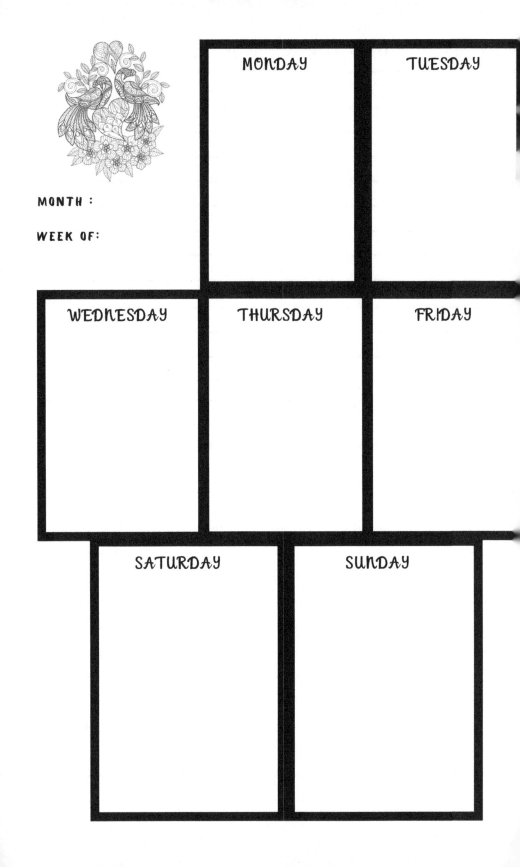

MONTH :

WEEK OF:

MONDAY

TUESDAY

WEDNESDAY

THURSDAY

FRIDAY

SATURDAY

SUNDAY

This Week's Shit List

Other Shit To Remember

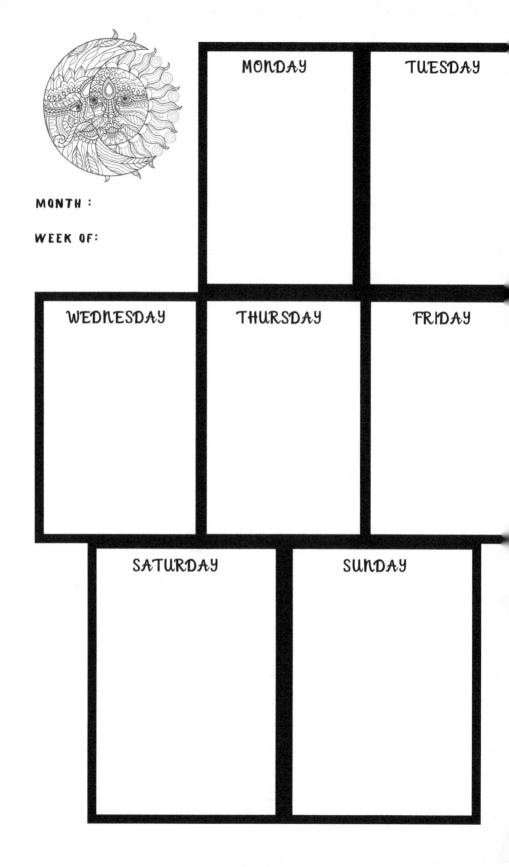

MONTH :

WEEK OF:

MONDAY

TUESDAY

WEDNESDAY

THURSDAY

FRIDAY

SATURDAY

SUNDAY

This Week's Shit List

Other Shit To Remember

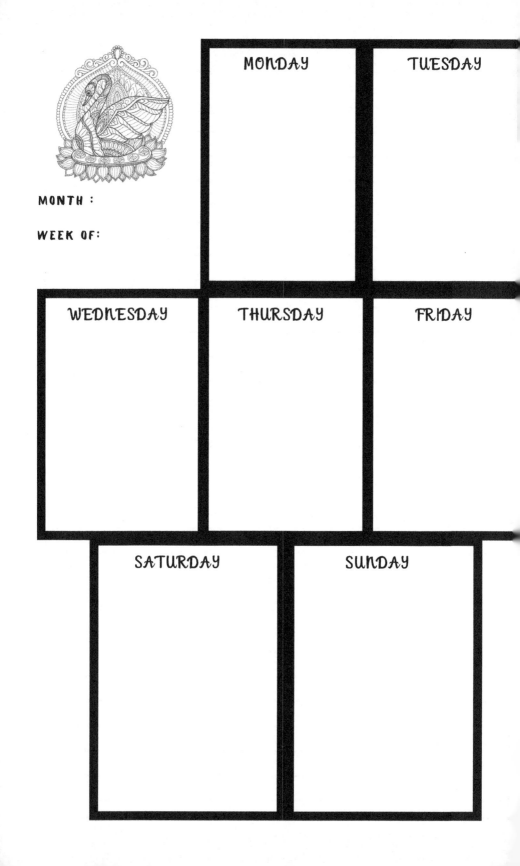

MONTH :

WEEK OF:

MONDAY

TUESDAY

WEDNESDAY

THURSDAY

FRIDAY

SATURDAY

SUNDAY

This Week's Shit List

Other Shit To Remember

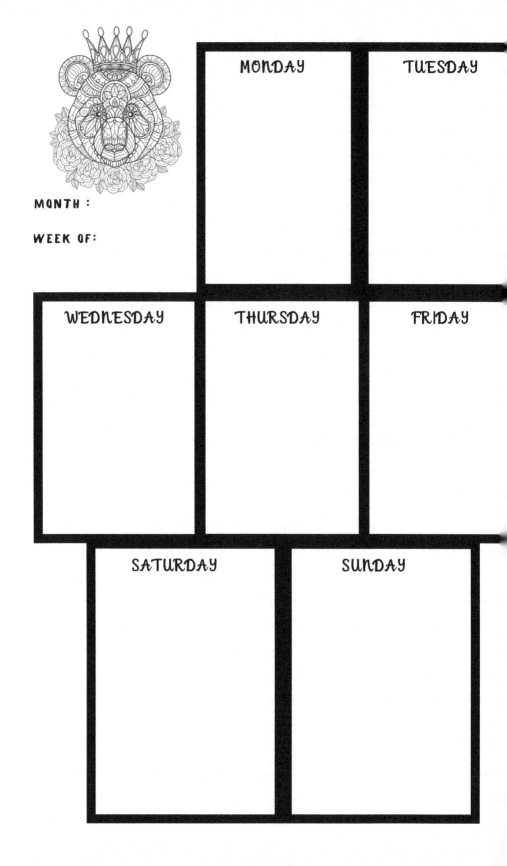

MONTH :

WEEK OF:

MONDAY

TUESDAY

WEDNESDAY

THURSDAY

FRIDAY

SATURDAY

SUNDAY

This Week's Shit List

Other Shit To Remember

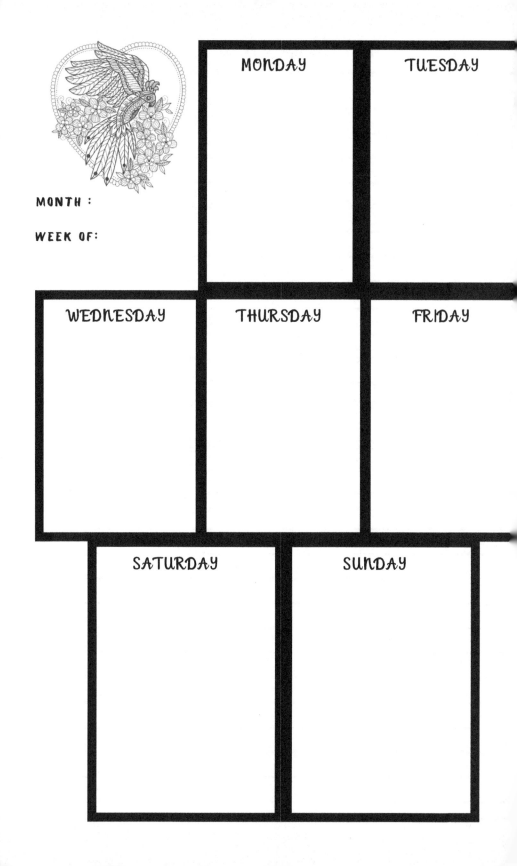

MONTH :

WEEK OF:

MONDAY

TUESDAY

WEDNESDAY

THURSDAY

FRIDAY

SATURDAY

SUNDAY

This Week's Shit List

Other Shit To Remember

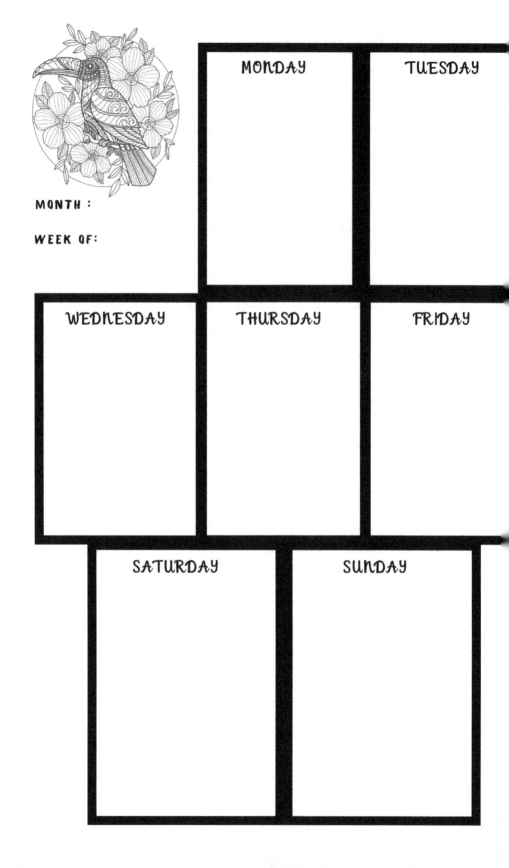

MONTH :

WEEK OF:

MONDAY

TUESDAY

WEDNESDAY

THURSDAY

FRIDAY

SATURDAY

SUNDAY

This Week's Shit List

Other Shit To Remember

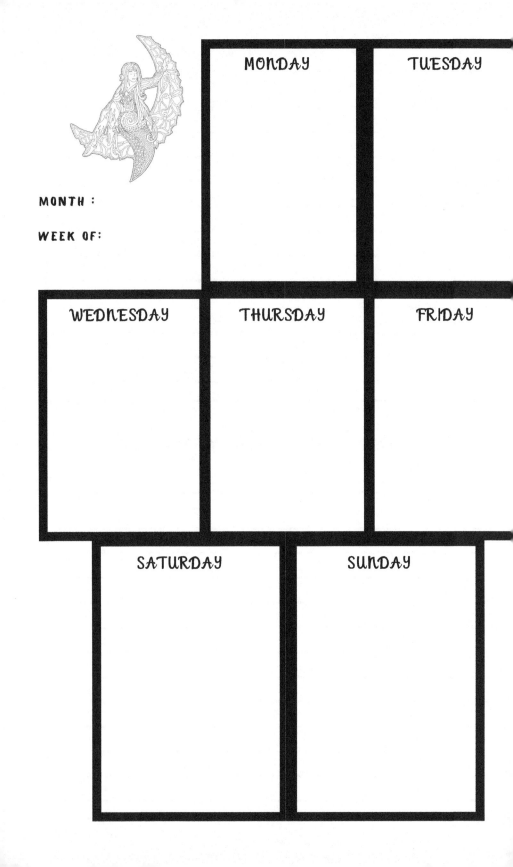

MONTH :

WEEK OF:

MONDAY

TUESDAY

WEDNESDAY

THURSDAY

FRIDAY

SATURDAY

SUNDAY

This Week's Shit List

Other Shit To Remember

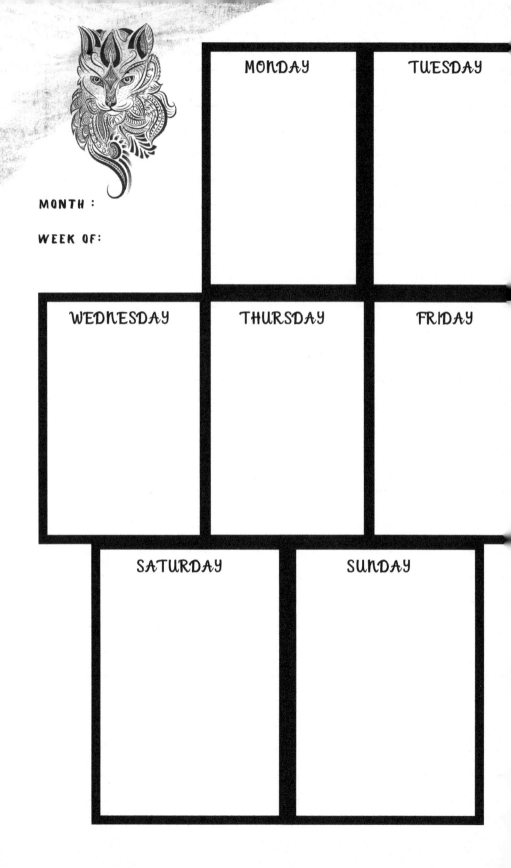

MONTH :

WEEK OF:

MONDAY

TUESDAY

WEDNESDAY

THURSDAY

FRIDAY

SATURDAY

SUNDAY

This Week's Shit List

_____
_____
_____
_____
_____
_____
_____
_____
_____
_____
_____

Other Shit To Remember

_____
_____
_____
_____
_____
_____
_____
_____
_____
_____

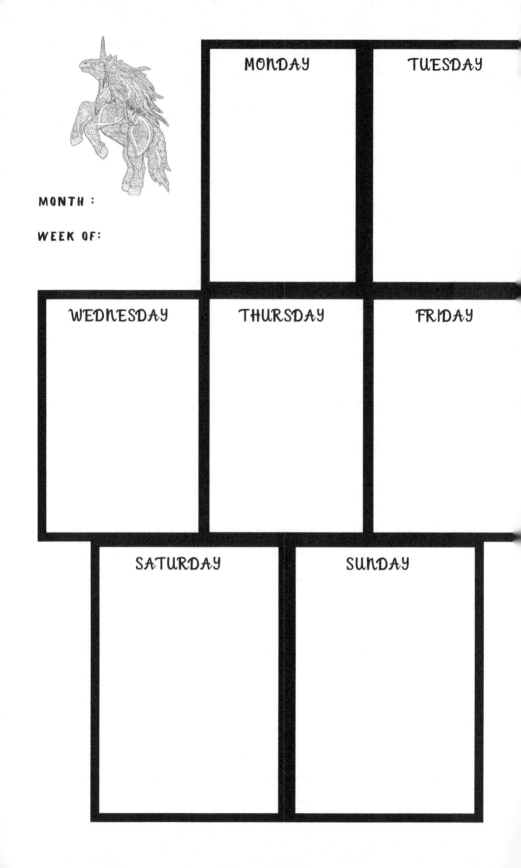

MONTH :

WEEK OF:

MONDAY

TUESDAY

WEDNESDAY

THURSDAY

FRIDAY

SATURDAY

SUNDAY

This Week's Shit List

_____
_____
_____
_____
_____
_____
_____
_____
_____
_____
_____
_____
_____
_____

Other Shit To Remember

_____
_____
_____
_____
_____
_____
_____
_____
_____
_____
_____
_____
_____

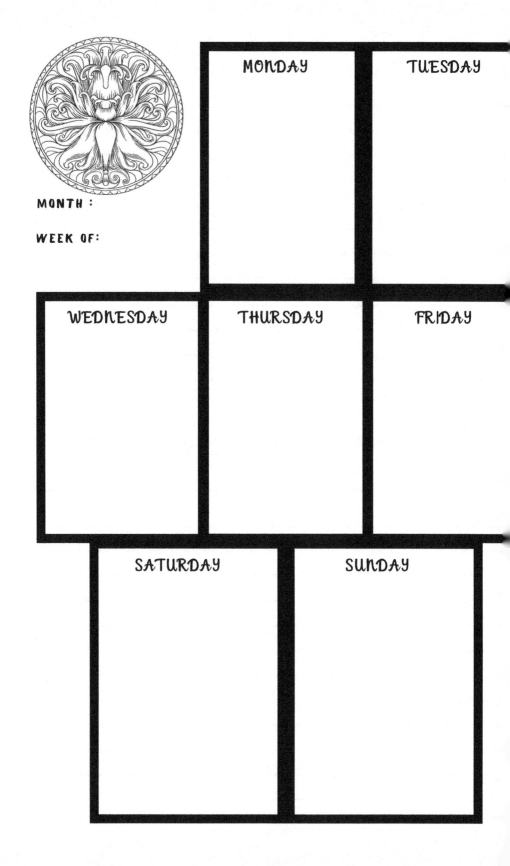

MONTH :

WEEK OF:

MONDAY

TUESDAY

WEDNESDAY

THURSDAY

FRIDAY

SATURDAY

SUNDAY

This Week's Shit List

Other Shit To Remember

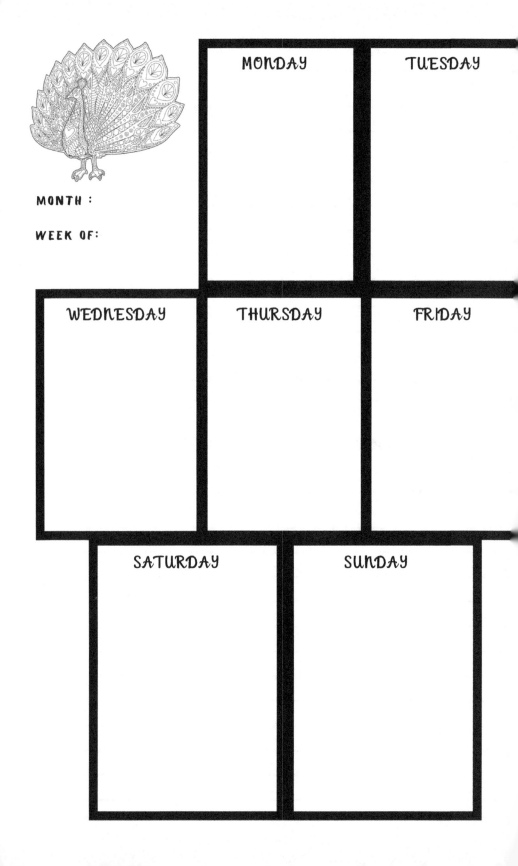

MONTH :

WEEK OF:

MONDAY

TUESDAY

WEDNESDAY

THURSDAY

FRIDAY

SATURDAY

SUNDAY

This Week's Shit List

Other Shit To Remember

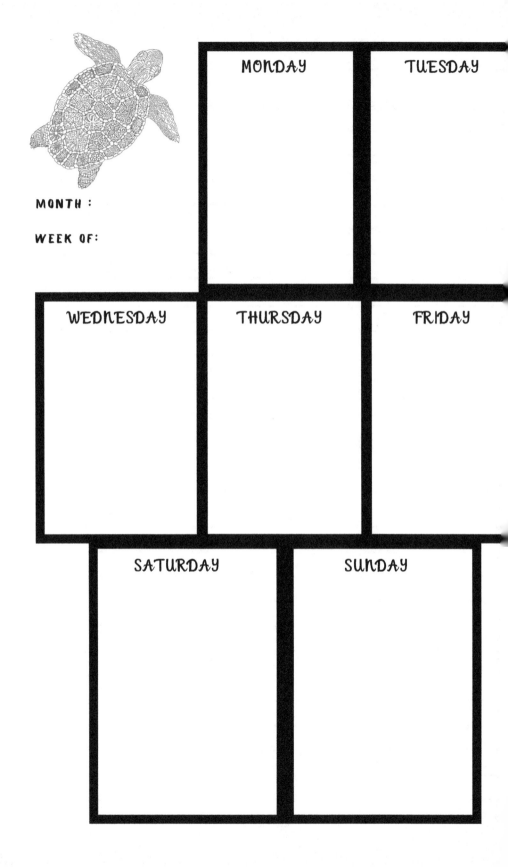

MONTH :

WEEK OF:

MONDAY

TUESDAY

WEDNESDAY

THURSDAY

FRIDAY

SATURDAY

SUNDAY

This Week's Shit List

Other Shit To Remember

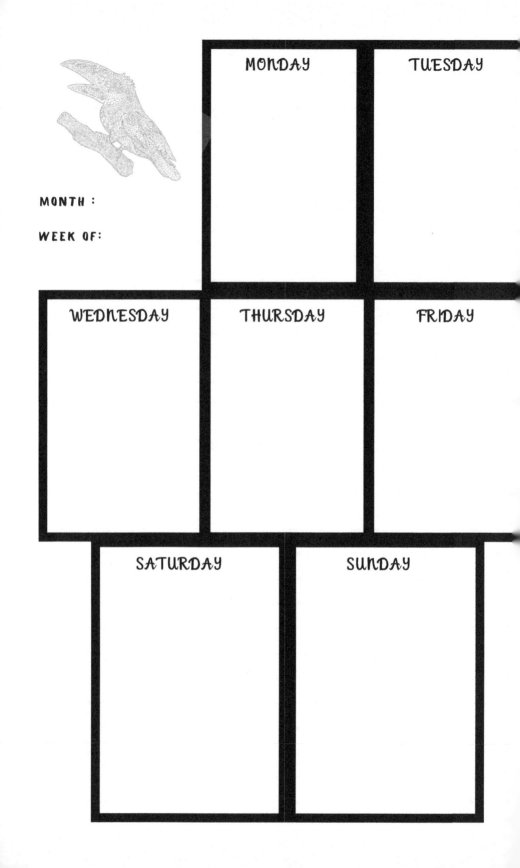

MONTH :

WEEK OF:

MONDAY

TUESDAY

WEDNESDAY

THURSDAY

FRIDAY

SATURDAY

SUNDAY

This Week's Shit List

Other Shit To Remember

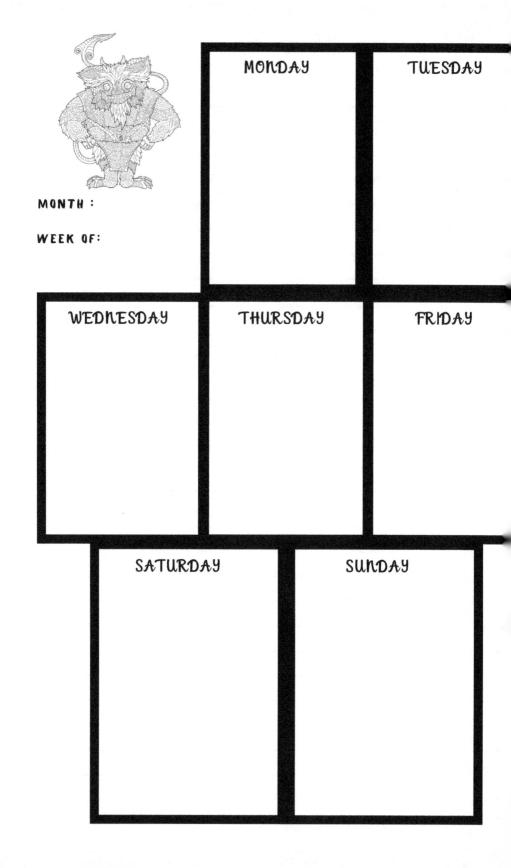

MONTH :

WEEK OF:

MONDAY

TUESDAY

WEDNESDAY

THURSDAY

FRIDAY

SATURDAY

SUNDAY

This Week's Shit List

Other Shit To Remember

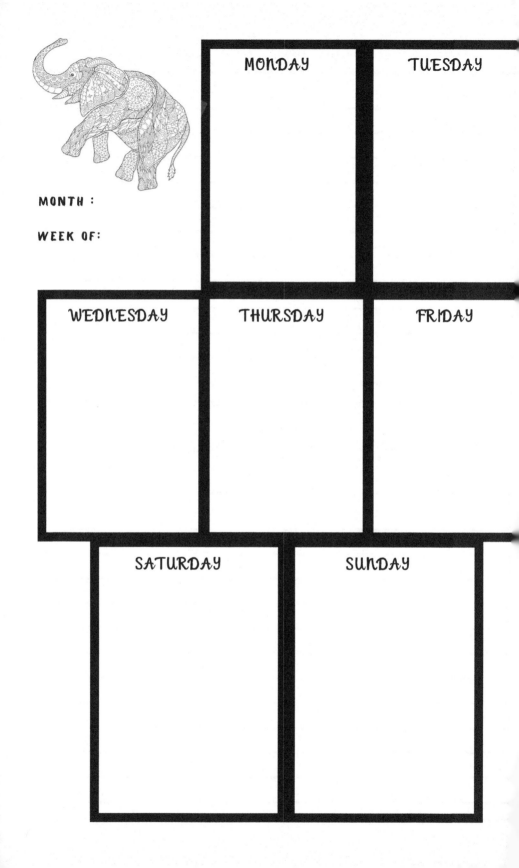

MONTH :

WEEK OF:

MONDAY

TUESDAY

WEDNESDAY

THURSDAY

FRIDAY

SATURDAY

SUNDAY

This Week's Shit List

Other Shit To Remember

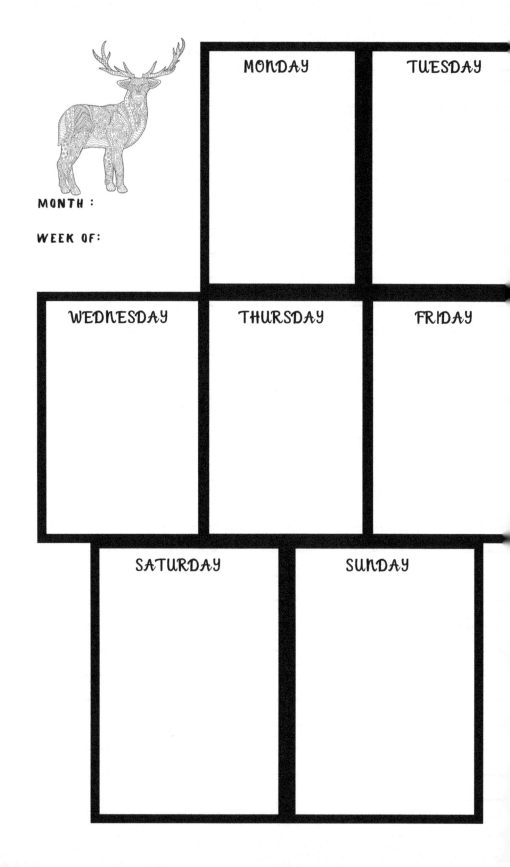

MONTH :

WEEK OF:

MONDAY

TUESDAY

WEDNESDAY

THURSDAY

FRIDAY

SATURDAY

SUNDAY

This Week's Shit List

Other Shit To Remember

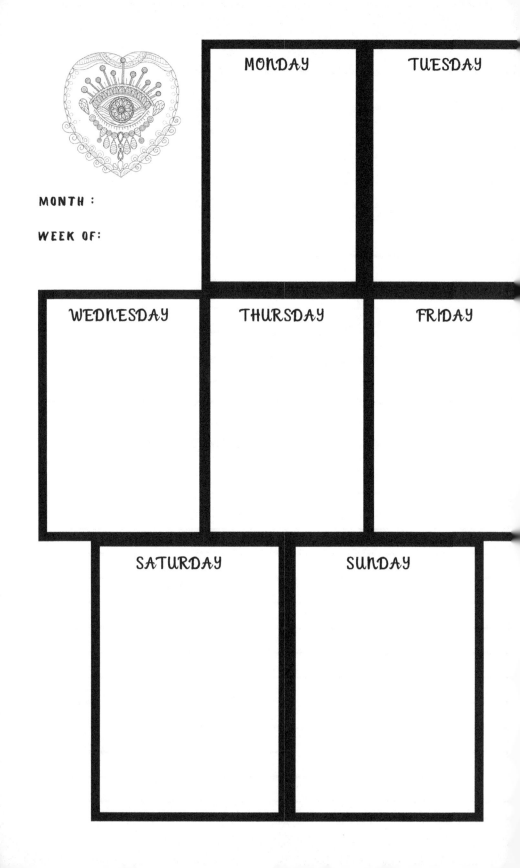

MONTH :

WEEK OF:

MONDAY

TUESDAY

WEDNESDAY

THURSDAY

FRIDAY

SATURDAY

SUNDAY

This Week's Shit List

Other Shit To Remember

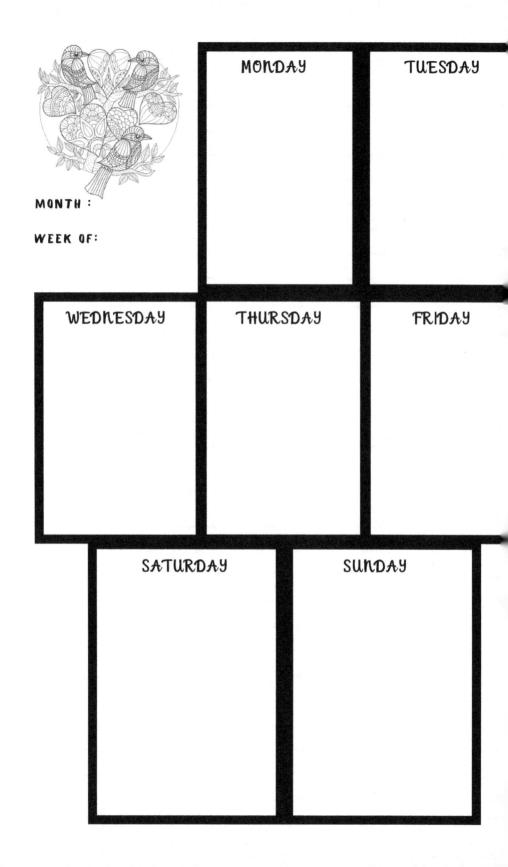

MONTH :

WEEK OF:

MONDAY

TUESDAY

WEDNESDAY

THURSDAY

FRIDAY

SATURDAY

SUNDAY

This Week's Shit List

Other Shit To Remember

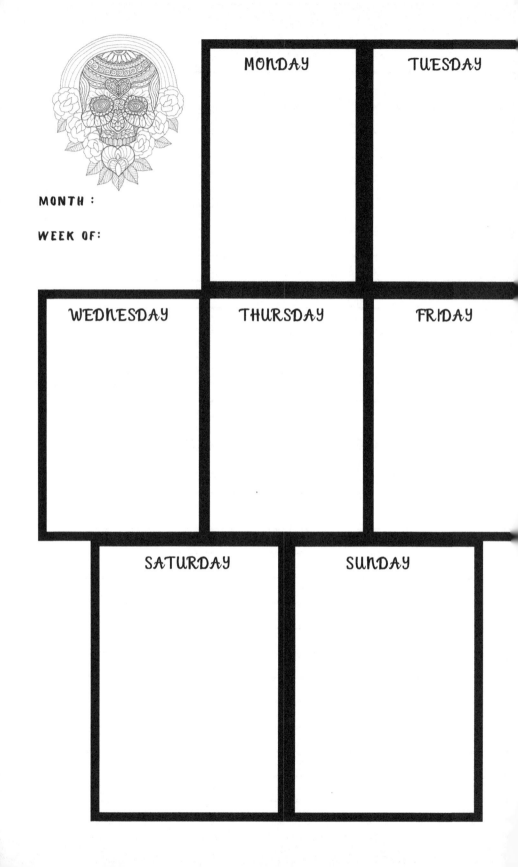

MONTH :

WEEK OF:

MONDAY

TUESDAY

WEDNESDAY

THURSDAY

FRIDAY

SATURDAY

SUNDAY

This Week's Shit List

Other Shit To Remember

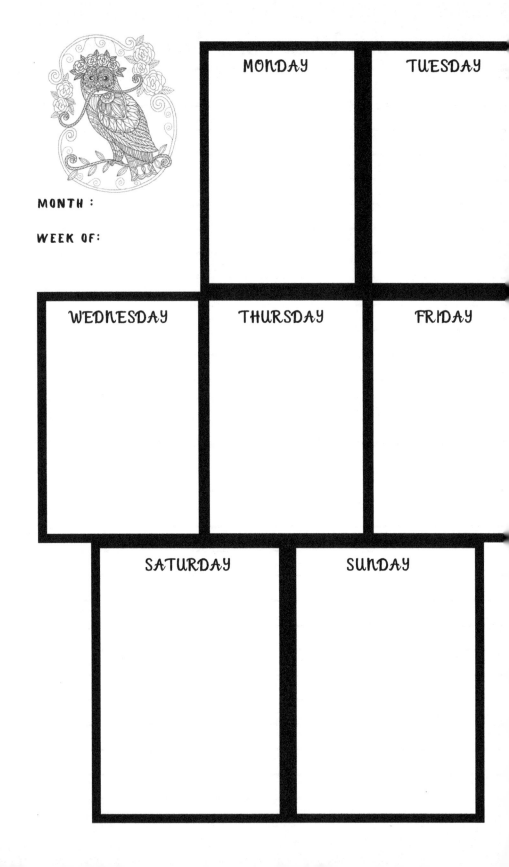

MONTH :

WEEK OF:

MONDAY

TUESDAY

WEDNESDAY

THURSDAY

FRIDAY

SATURDAY

SUNDAY

This Week's Shit List

_____

_____

_____

_____

_____

_____

_____

_____

_____

Other Shit To Remember

_____

_____

_____

_____

_____

_____

_____

_____

_____

_____

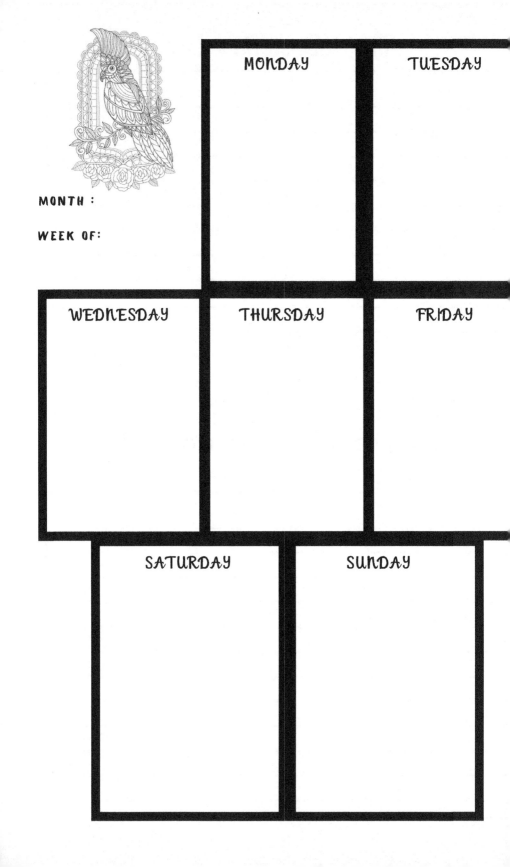

MONTH :

WEEK OF:

MONDAY

TUESDAY

WEDNESDAY

THURSDAY

FRIDAY

SATURDAY

SUNDAY

This Week's Shit List

Other Shit To Remember

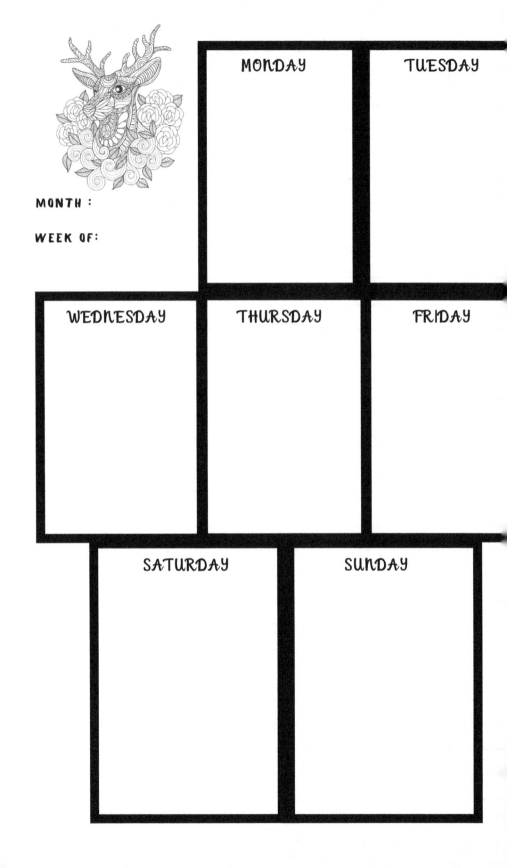

MONTH :

WEEK OF:

MONDAY

TUESDAY

WEDNESDAY

THURSDAY

FRIDAY

SATURDAY

SUNDAY

This Week's Shit List

_____
_____
_____
_____
_____
_____
_____
_____
_____
_____
_____
_____

Other Shit To Remember

_____
_____
_____
_____
_____
_____
_____
_____
_____
_____
_____

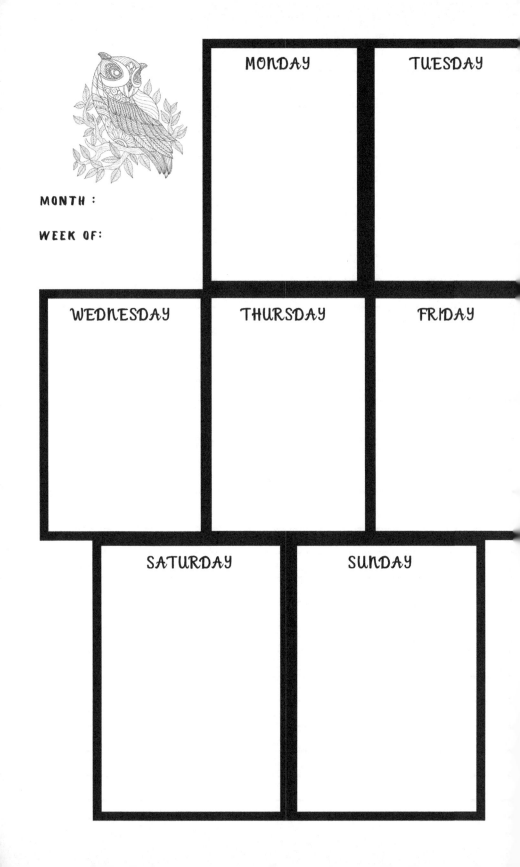

MONTH :

WEEK OF:

MONDAY

TUESDAY

WEDNESDAY

THURSDAY

FRIDAY

SATURDAY

SUNDAY

This Week's Shit List

Other Shit To Remember

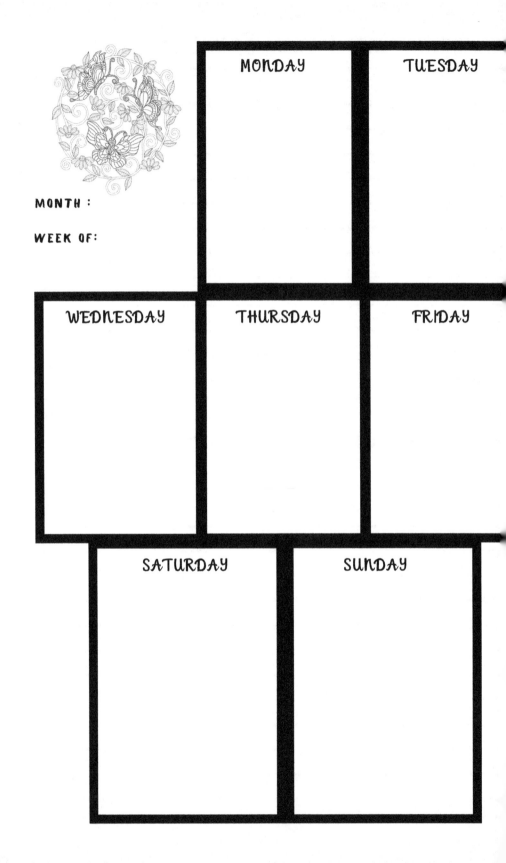

MONTH :

WEEK OF:

MONDAY

TUESDAY

WEDNESDAY

THURSDAY

FRIDAY

SATURDAY

SUNDAY

This Week's Shit List

_____
_____
_____
_____
_____
_____
_____
_____
_____
_____
_____
_____
_____
_____

Other Shit To Remember

_____
_____
_____
_____
_____
_____
_____
_____
_____
_____
_____
_____
_____
_____
_____

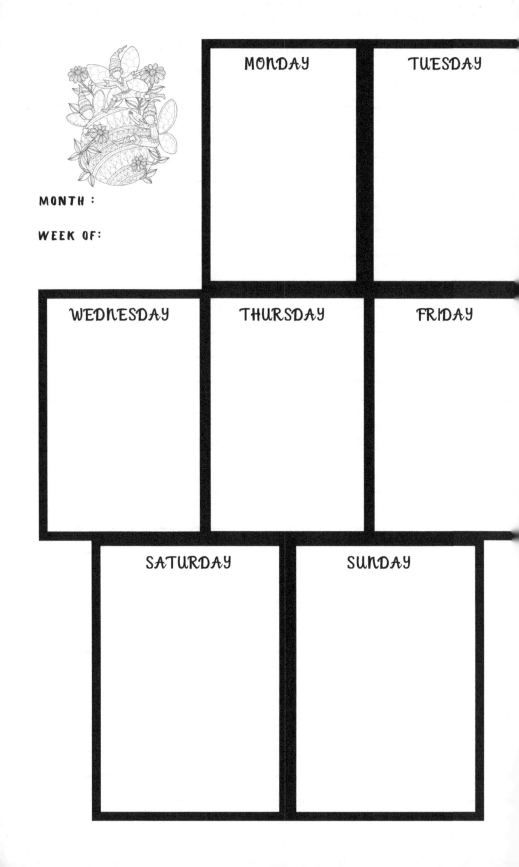

MONTH :

WEEK OF:

MONDAY

TUESDAY

WEDNESDAY

THURSDAY

FRIDAY

SATURDAY

SUNDAY

This Week's Shit List

Other Shit To Remember

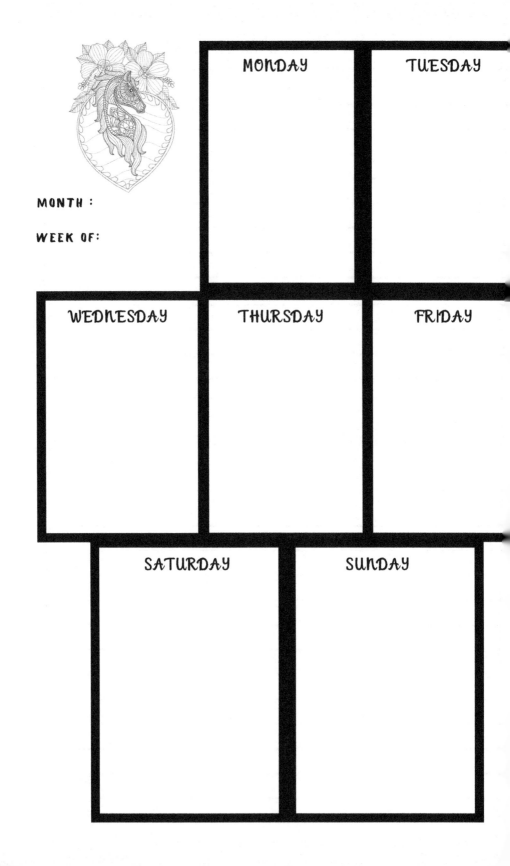

MONTH :

WEEK OF:

MONDAY

TUESDAY

WEDNESDAY

THURSDAY

FRIDAY

SATURDAY

SUNDAY

This Week's Shit List

Other Shit To Remember

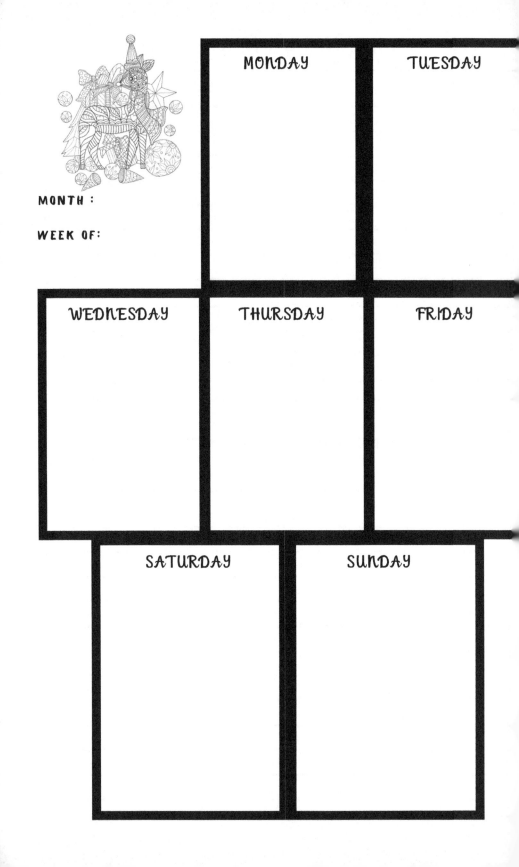

MONTH :

WEEK OF:

MONDAY

TUESDAY

WEDNESDAY

THURSDAY

FRIDAY

SATURDAY

SUNDAY

This Week's Shit List

Other Shit To Remember

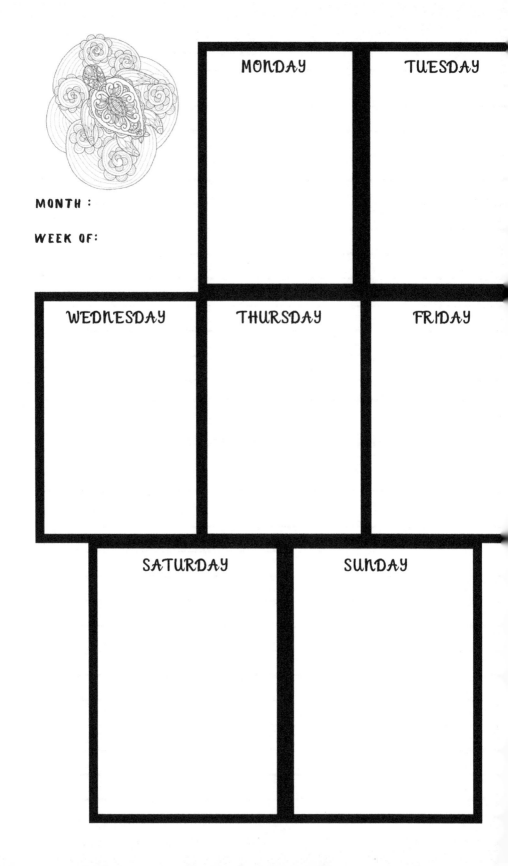

MONTH :

WEEK OF:

MONDAY

TUESDAY

WEDNESDAY

THURSDAY

FRIDAY

SATURDAY

SUNDAY

This Week's Shit List

Other Shit To Remember

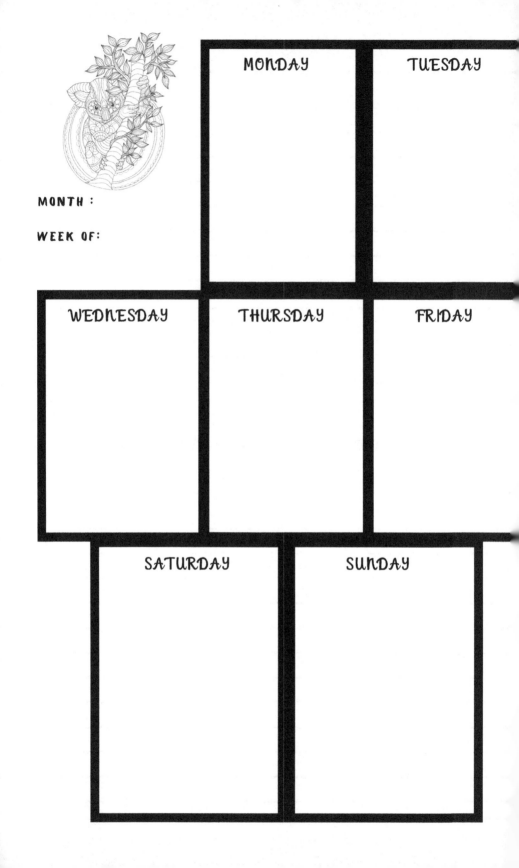

MONTH :

WEEK OF:

MONDAY

TUESDAY

WEDNESDAY

THURSDAY

FRIDAY

SATURDAY

SUNDAY

This Week's Shit List

Other Shit To Remember

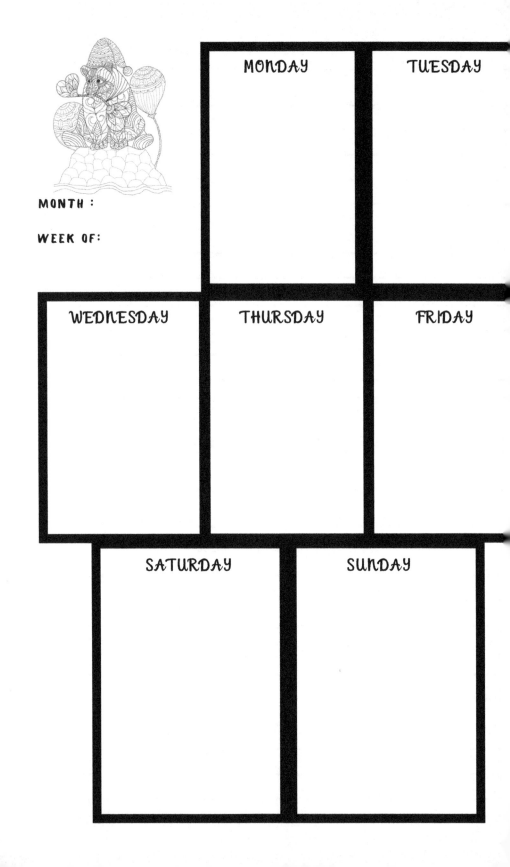

MONTH :

WEEK OF:

MONDAY

TUESDAY

WEDNESDAY

THURSDAY

FRIDAY

SATURDAY

SUNDAY

This Week's Shit List

Other Shit To Remember

Thank You

We hope that you
found this book useful.
And we remind you to
leave us a five stars review
to help us grow our store

Made in the USA
Las Vegas, NV
06 December 2021

36287428R00057